MUSICAL
INSTRUM

Created by Gallimard Jeunesse
and Claude Delafosse
Illustrated by Donald Grant

A FIRST DISCOVERY BOOK

Cartwheel
·B·O·O·K·S· ®
SCHOLASTIC INC.
New York   Toronto   London   Auckland   Sydney

Leaves rustle   Thunder booms   Waterfalls roar

Listen to the musical
sounds of nature.
What do you hear?

Sounds are made by
rapid movements called
vibrations.

Bees
buzz

Wood-
peckers
peck

Crickets
chirp

People around the world make many
different kinds of musical instruments.
You can even make and play
some simple instruments at home.

Cats
meow

Some
instruments
are
made by
skilled
artisans.

Dogs bark

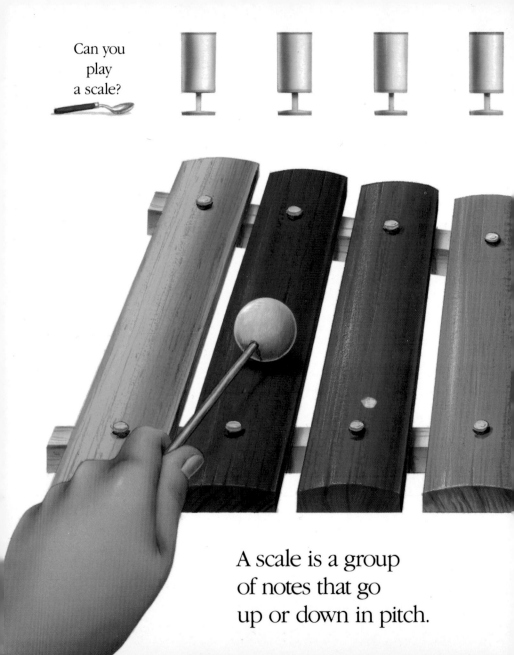

Can you play a scale?

A scale is a group of notes that go up or down in pitch.

Can you make this instrument?

Fill eight glasses with increasing amounts of water.
Tap each with a spoon.
Which glasses make the higher sounds?
(the ones with more water)

Which bars on a xylophone
make the higher sounds when struck
with a mallet? (the shorter ones)

Pianos come
in different sizes.
A grand piano
is usually used
in concerts.

A piano keyboard has 88 keys.
Some are white and some are black.

When you press a key, you lift a padded hammer hidden inside
the piano. The hammer strikes a piano string and makes a sound.
The shorter strings make the higher notes.

These instruments are members of the string family.

The bow, made with horsehair, is used to play these instruments.

The strings vibrate and make sounds when you draw the bow across them.

Thinner strings and smaller instruments make higher sounds.

Violin

Viola

String players can also pluck the strings. The term for plucking the strings is *pizzicato*.

Cello

Bass

This stringed instrument is an acoustic or classic guitar.

When you pluck or strum a string, it vibrates and makes a sound. The sound is made louder or "amplified" inside the hollow body of the guitar.

This is an electric guitar.

Guitar pick

This electric guitar has a solid body. It is connected to an amplifier by an electrical cord. An electric amplifier can make the sound *very* loud.

Nasal flute

Japanese flute

Piccolo

Double Bedouin clarinet

Flageolet

Wind instruments produce sound from the vibration of air in a tube or pipe.

Flute

A flute has holes along the side. The holes have little caps called keys that you can press down.

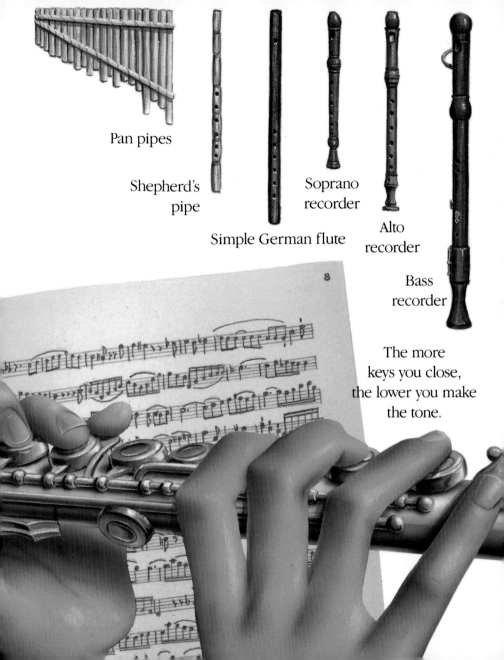

Pan pipes

Shepherd's pipe

Simple German flute

Soprano recorder

Alto recorder

Bass recorder

The more keys you close, the lower you make the tone.

Meet the reed family!

Have you ever made a whistle by blowing on a blade of grass? You also can make music by blowing on a reed in a reed instrument.

Clarinet   Oboe

Bassoon

Soprano saxophone

Trumpet

Meet the brass family, too!

Sousaphone

By changing lip
pressure and
pressing valves, you can
make different sounds.

With brass instruments,
the musician's lips vibrate.

Percussion
instruments
provide rhythm —
they play the beat.

You either strike
them or
shake them.

You might find
this drum set
in a jazz or
rock-'n'-roll
band.

Can you find
six drums and
the cymbals?

A symphony orchestra
contains many different
kinds of instruments
and musicians.

Drums

Vibraphone

French
horns

Trumpets

Flutes

Clarinets

Harp

First violins

Second violins

Concert master

Timpáni

Triangle

Cymbals

Tubas

Trombones

Oboes

Bassoons

Bass viols

Violas

Cellos

Because it contains so many different instruments, an orchestra can create a great variety of musical sounds.

A conductor leads the musicians. He holds a baton.

Latin-
American
maracas

Scottish
bagpipes

Indian sitar

Some musical
instruments
are associated
with certain
regions.

American
banjo

Lapland
flute

Spanish
castanets

German
harmonica

Swiss
bells

Kora of Mali

Amazon
flute

Here are some instruments you can make.

Stretch rubber bands around a box to make a homemade guitar.

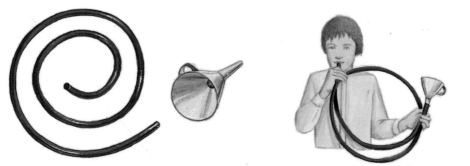

Blow into a tube with a funnel at the end to make a wind instrument.

Put dried beans and unpopped popcorn in jars to make shakers.

What songs can you play?

Your hands are a percussion
instrument. What rhythms can you clap?
Your voice is a musical instrument, too.
Put your hand on your throat and sing.
What do you feel? Vibrations!

Titles in the series of *First Discovery Books:*

**Airplanes
and Flying Machines**
All About Time
Bears
*****Birds**
*****Boats**
*****The Camera**
**Cars and Trucks
and Other Vehicles**
*****Castles**
Cats
Colors
Dinosaurs
The Earth and Sky
******The Egg**
Flowers

Fruit
The Human Body
**The Ladybug and
Other Insects**
Light
Musical Instruments
Penguins
Pyramids
The Rain Forest
*****The River**
The Seashore
*******The Tree**
Under the Ground
**Vegetables in the
Garden**
Water
********Weather**
*****Whales**

Titles in the series of *First Discovery Art Books:*

Animals
Landscapes
Paintings
Portraits

Titles in the series of *First Discovery Atlas Books:*

Atlas of Animals
Atlas of Countries
Atlas of People
Atlas of Plants

*Parents Magazine
"Best Books" Award

**Parenting Magazine
Reading Magic Award

***Oppenheim Toy Portfolio
Gold Seal Award

Library of Congress Cataloging-in-Publication Data available.
Originally published in France under the title LA MUSIQUE by Editions Gallimard.

ISBN 0-590-47729-3
Text copyright © 1992 by Editions Gallimard.
This edition English translation by Jennifer Riggs.
This edition American text by Jean Marzollo.
All rights reserved. First published in the U.S.A. in 1994 by Scholastic Inc. by arrangement with Editions Gallimard.
CARTWHEEL BOOKS ® is a registered trademark of Scholastic Inc.
12 11 10 9 8 7 6 5 4   6 7 8 9/9
Printed in Italy
First Scholastic printing, March 1994